THIS JOURNAL BELONGS TO
THE WRECKER

Renee Tiwari

WRITE YOUR NAME USING LARGE LETTERS

WRITE YOUR NAME WITH TINY LETTERS

WRITE YOUR NAME BACKWARD

WRITE YOUR NAME AS AN AUTOGRAPH

Renee Tiwari

WRITE YOUR NAME USING A COLOR

ADDRESS:

PHONE NUMBER:

----

*IF FOUND, FLIP TO A PAGE OF YOUR CHOICE, FOLLOW THE INSTRUCTIONS
THEN RETURN TO THE OWNER

WRECK THIS JOURNAL

"YOU WIN SOME
YOU LOSE SOME
YOU WRECK SOME"

DALE EARNHARDT

WARNING:

WRECKING THIS BOOK MIGHT GET YOU DIRTY. YOU MAY FIND YOURSELF COVERED IN PAINT, DIRT, FOREIGN SUBSTANCES, OR STICKY FINGERS. THAT MEANS YOU'RE WRECKING THE JOURNAL IN A GOOD WAY, NOT THAT THERE IS ANY GOOD WAY.

BE CREATIVE, BE RECKLESS, AND LET YOUR IMAGINATION TAKE CONTROL. DON'T GRIEVE FOR THE JOURNAL'S PERFECT STATE FROM THE BEGINNING YET ENJOY THE WRECKED STATE FROM THE END.

DEAR WRECKER, THIS JOURNAL WAS MADE TO BE USED NO MATTER WHERE YOU FIND YOURSELF. JUST KEEP IN MIND TO HAVE AS MUCH FUN AS YOU CAN WHILE COMPLETING THE TASKS. IT'S TIME TO START AN ADVENTURE. SO STOP READING AND START WRECKING.
HAPPY WRECKING!

1. Try to carry the journal with you everywhere you go.

2. Follow the instructions on every page.

3. The order it's not important.

4. Instructions are open to interpretation.

5. Experiment on each task (work against your better judgment).

materials

ideas	emotions
paint	photos
glue	tea
dirt	coffee
water	fears
saliva	food
garbage	scissors
pencil	tape
stamps	time
stickers	spontaneity
pen	sharp things
unpredictability	magazines
grease	stapler
detergent	wax
string	ink
office supplies	shoes
grass	tissues
spoons	newspaper
needle	gum
straw	sponge
ball	matches

YOU MAY ADD YOUR OWN PAGE NUMBERS.

starting here

FIND A WAY TO CARRY THE JOURNAL EVERYWHERE YOU GO

Create a nonstop line

(use Pen, Pencil, marker, nail Polish...)

Fill this page
with your
favorite color

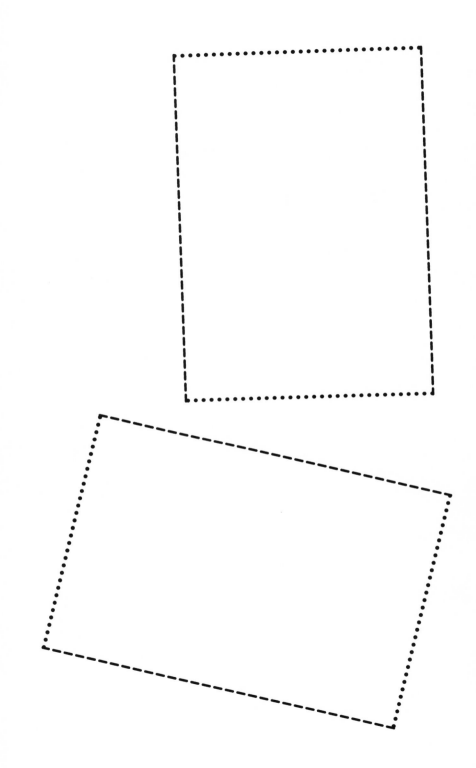

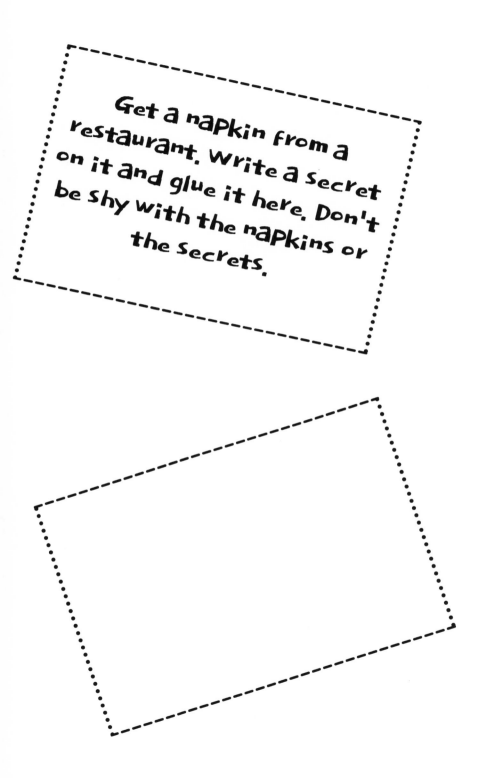

Get a napkin from a restaurant. Write a secret on it and glue it here. Don't be shy with the napkins or the secrets.

A page for five letter
WORDS
(write or glue cut words)

Get some cat or dog paws on these pages

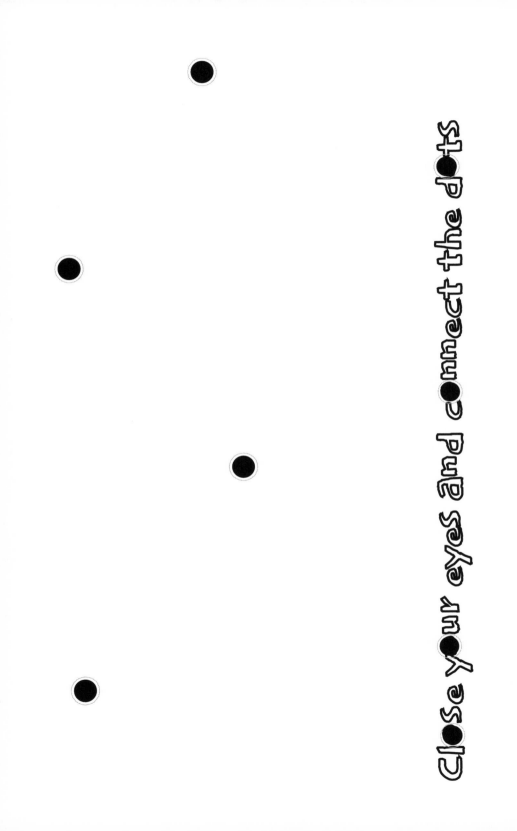

Close your eyes and connect the dots

Pages of good
thoughts

Draw directions to your favorite Place in town

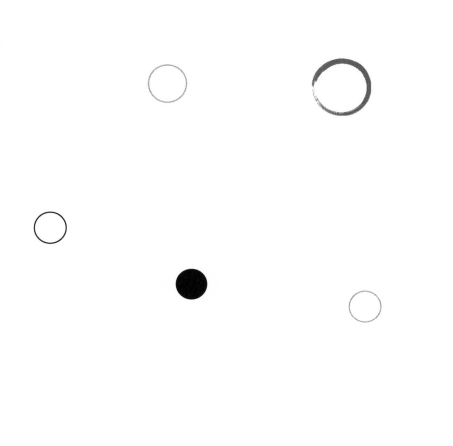

Choose your own
wrecking method

~~~~~~

~~~~~~

Date ~~~~~~~~   Sign ~~~~~~~~

Make a
mess and
clean it up

COVER
THESE
PAGES WITH
STICKER
NOTES

TRACE THE THINGS FROM
YOUR BAG OR POCKETS

FILL THIS SPACE WHILE
DREAMING OUTSIDE

(you find them on bought fruits)

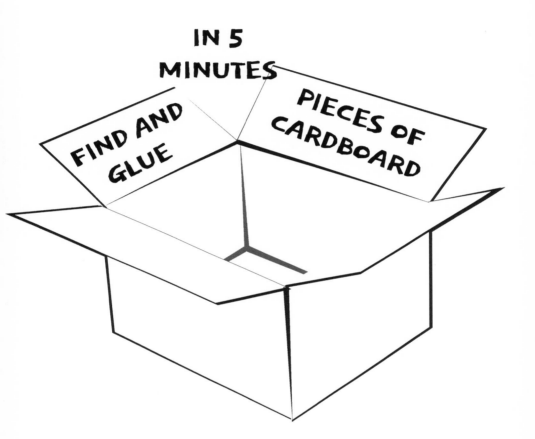

PICK UP THE JOURNAL

WITHOUT USING YOUR HANDS

(draw how you did it)

Choose your own
wrecking method

Date ---------   Sign ---------

TIE A STRING TO THE JOURNAL

GO FOR A WALK AND DRAG IT

PLACE STICKY THINGS HERE

DRIP SOMETHING HERE

(ink, coffee, paint and close the book to make a print)

SEW THIS PAGE

Choose your own
wrecking method

~~~~~~

~~~~~~

Date ~~~~~~~~~   Sign ~~~~~~~~~

DRAW LINES

(thin, fat, dashed lines)

MODERN PAINTING

(make a trace of your hand or feet or both)

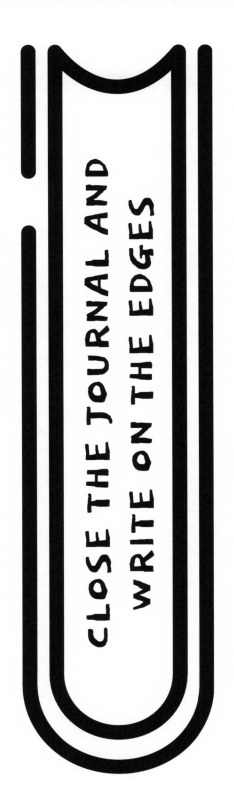

CLOSE THE JOURNAL AND WRITE ON THE EDGES

USE THIS AS A PAGE
TEST FOR COLORS

COVER THESE PAGES USING
ONLY ITEMS FOUND IN THE
OUTDOORS

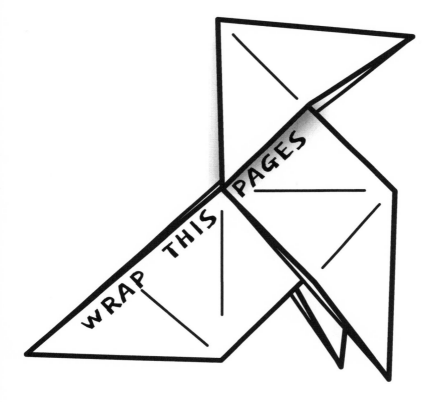

THROW OBJECTS ON THE TARGET

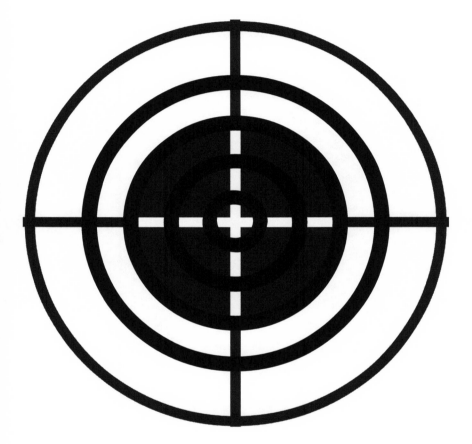

(make sure you leave marks, dents, paint, dirt...)

MAKE A
COLLECTION OF
LEAFS

Choose your own wrecking method

_____

_____

Date _____   Sign _____

COLLECT DEAD BUGS

FILL THIS PAGE WITH COUPONS, DISCOUNT CODES, SALES

WRITE EVERY WORD ON THIS PAGE BACKWARD

FREEZE THIS PAGE

PAGE WITH ARTICLES FROM A MAGAZINE

SHARPEN YOUR PENCIL HERE

Choose your own wrecking method

Date _____   Sign _____

TAKE A WALK ON WET GRASS THEN STAND HERE

(jump up and down)

COLLECT NAMES, AUTOGRAPHS, AND PEOPLES DREAMS

dream

FIND TEN VERY SMALL ITEMS TO
GLUE HERE

WRITE OR DRAW WHAT YOU SEE AROUND YOU

(while you wait for the bus, metro, plane, food, etc)

MAKE FRUITS OR VEGETABLE STAMPS

COLLECT YOUR POCKET LINT
(and glue it here)

DOCUMENT IN DETAIL A VERY EXCITING ADVENTURE

COLLECT NUMBERS

Choose your own wrecking method

Date _____   Sign _____

PAINT USING
ABNORMAL OBJECTS
(spoon, fork, hair, plants)

FIND A WAY
TO WEAR
THIS
JOURNAL

DRAW A TREASURE MAP

PAINT USING ONLY YOUR FEET

DOCUMENT
YOUR MEALS

(rub, smear, splatter your food, use this
page as a napkin)

TEAR IT UP!

RIP STRIPS!

ASK A FRIEND TO DO
SOMETHING DISTRUCTIVE TO
THIS PAGE

ALSO FROM
COLOR DOE SMILE

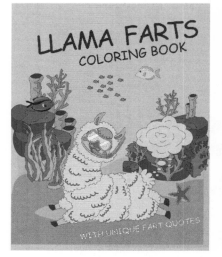

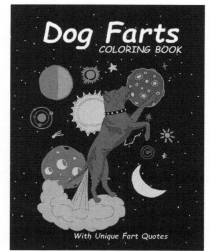

STARTED

FINISHED